ideals®
CHRISTMAS

Hold to your eye
the colors of Christmas:
flame of poinsettia, holly's red,
spicy greens and the candles' glow,
bright papers and ribbons,
a hundred cards,
and a cathedral's hushed, dim nave.

Hold to your ear
the sounds of the season:
Christmas carols from a dozen lands,
joyous bells and their pealing,
organ and choir and a child's high voice,
the silence of snowfall late at night.

Hold to your heart, O hold to your heart
the unchanging dream of Christmas:
the shining Star that led Wise Men on
to a Babe in his mother's arms,
and, all about, the angels praying
as we must pray, as we all must pray,
"Peace on earth; good will to all men."

Elizabeth Searle Lamb

Editorial Director, James Kuse

Managing Editor, Ralph Luedtke

Associate Editor, Colleen Callahan Gonring

Production Editor/Manager, Richard Lawson

Photographic Editor, Gerald Koser

Copy Editor, Sharon Style

IDEALS—Vol. 36 No. 8 November MCMLXXIX, IDEALS (ISSN 0019-137X) is published eight times a year,
January, February, April, June, July, September, October, November
by IDEALS PUBLISHING CORPORATION, 11315 Watertown Plank Road, Milwaukee, Wis. 53226
Second class postage paid at Milwaukee, Wisconsin. Copyright ©MCMLXXIX by IDEALS PUBLISHING CORPORATION.
Postmaster, please send form 3579 to Ideals Publishing Corporation. 175 Community Drive. Great Neck, New York, 11025
All rights reserved. Title IDEALS registered U.S. Patent Office.
Published Simultaneously in Canada

ONE YEAR SUBSCRIPTION—eight consecutive issues as published—only $15.95
TWO YEAR SUBSCRIPTION—sixteen consecutive issues as published—only $27.95
SINGLE ISSUES—only $2.95

ISBN 0-89542-328-6 295

Let Us Be Quiet

Let us be still awhile this Christmastime;
O hurrying hearts restrain your restless beat;
Let us go journeying on some upward climb
Into the pure air, rarefied and sweet,
With the memory of another far-off night
When the Christ was born beneath a star's white light.

We have been loud and boisterous far too long,
Let us be silent, and perhaps we will,
By listening, hear the angels's heralding song
Ring clearly out above some distant hill,
And if we leave the clamoring word unsaid
A voice will guide us to Christ's manger bed.

It was a silent night, the night He came,
A holy night and may we keep it so;
There is one star God's own hand set aflame,
Its lengthening rays will guide us as we go;
It is a silent fire, its rays point far
And through the centuries they will not dim
For every silver line of light directs
Mankind on the shining road that leads to Him.

Grace Noll Crowell

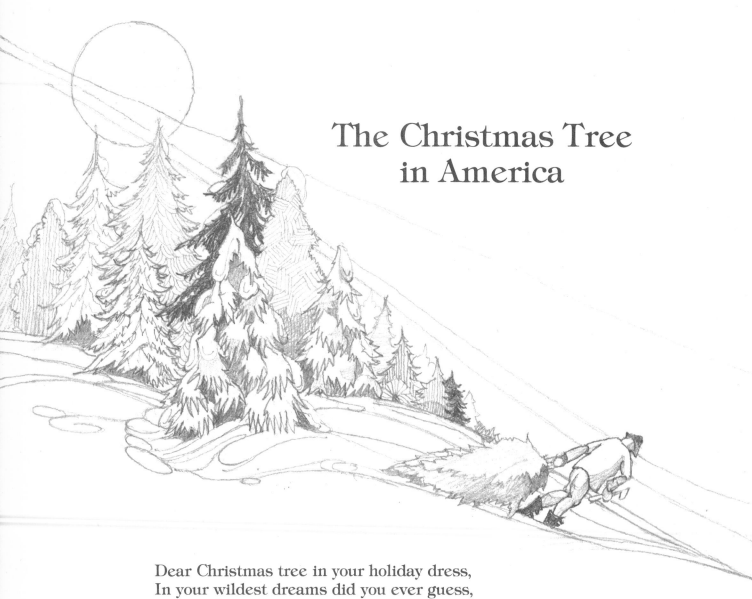

The Christmas Tree in America

Dear Christmas tree in your holiday dress,
In your wildest dreams did you ever guess,
In your forest home so far away,
That you would be standing here today

With a garland of gold around your waist,
All popcorn and cranberry encased,
With tinsel streamers, a star for a crown,
And all your branches weighted down

By baubles that sparkle and glitter and shine
And colored lightbulbs that entwine . . .
With all our "Ohs" and "Ahs" and sighs?
I bet it is a great surprise!

Jessie Cannon Eldridge

The tradition of "dressing" a tree for Christmas was introduced to Americans by German settlers and mercenaries in the early 1700s, but was not generally accepted until more than a century later. In 1845 Pennsylvania church publications began to reproduce Carl August Schwerdgeburth's portrayal of Martin Luther's family around a lighted Christmas tree. The work inspired pamphlets about the Christmas tree that soon became popular with Sunday School children. Both the painting and the pamphlets promoted the adoption of the Christmas tree as a religious symbol in American homes. Beginning with trees in homes here and there, the Christmas tree gained widespread popularity. Now, people of all denominations celebrate the Christmas holidays with a tree.

In nineteenth-century cities and larger towns, people dressed their trees with elaborate decorations. Fancy cookies and candies, gilt fruits and imported trinkets and miniature toys graced fir branches. Carefully placed candles illuminated the tree. What a grand occasion it must have been when a newly bedecked tree was finally unveiled to neighbors and children!

Families living in isolated cabins and rural settlements had simpler decorations. Ornaments and toys were often made from materials gathered in nearby woods or fields. Scraps saved from a calico dress or yarn left from mittens were fashioned into dolls. Clusters of nuts and pinecones nestled in branches draped with popcorn strings and gingerbread men. Perhaps it had less glitter, but the frontier tree must have been as proud as its city brother.

The Christmas Trees

There's a stir among the trees,
There's a whisper in the breeze,
Little ice-points clash and clink,
Little needles nod and wink,
Sturdy fir trees sway and sigh—
"Here am I! Here am I!"

"All the summer long I stood
In the silence of the woods.
Tall and tapering I grew;
What might happen well I knew;
For one day a little bird
Sang, and in the song I heard
Many things quite strange to me
Of Christmas and the Christmas tree.

"When the sun was hid from sight
In the darkness of the night,
When the wind with sudden fret
Pulled at my green coronet,
Staunch I stood, and hid my fears,
Weeping silent fragrant tears,
Praying still that I might be
Fitted for a Christmas tree.

"Now here we stand
On every hand!
In us a hoard of summer stored,
Birds have flown over us,
Blue sky has covered us,
Soft winds have sung to us,
Blossoms have flung to us
Measureless sweetness,
Now in completeness
We wait."

Mary Frances Butts

The Good Old Days

Christmas in the kitchen
was Mother's favorite room
where she would do her cooking
from morning, way till noon!

She was so very happy
with all the things she'd cook,
cookies, pies and puddings
all from Grandma's book.

Some of it for stockings,
and some for Christmas Day,
most of it for neighbors
that she would give away.

Come on now, let's all invade Grandma's kitchen around about this time of year. My, oh, my, what activity is going on there! Especially during the hours when kids are in school. The kitchen table is spread with a huge wooden breadboard covered with flour and here and there, you will see big yellow crockery bowls filled with different cookie mixes. I mean the homemade kind, not the kind young brides use today that come in a package. There will be plain sugar cookies that Mother can conveniently improvise and make all sorts of different kinds, some with raisins, some with nuts and some with cherries or even coconut. There might be gingerbread Santa Clauses, and some cut out like stars or angels. To one side will be another dish with different color frostings and tiny candies to top them off with. Now, all of these, Mother and Grandmother will stack away in their tin cans until Christmas to help fill the stockings.

On the old black kitchen stove you might see a big kettle steaming away with old coffee cans filled with suet puddings, a must for the holiday dinner.

Then, later, you might catch Grandmother rushing down to her preserve cellar for a couple of jars of mincemeat for her pies. This mincemeat was made in the early fall when Grandpa came home with a deer from hunting, which she soon chopped up for her mincemeat. Now fruitcake was another special necessity for Christmas and it was usually made a few weeks before Christmas to get mellow, as Grandmother used to say, and oftentimes we kids would help out by cutting up the cherries, raisins and citron to put in her mixture. Boy, was it good.!

Just before the holiday Mother would have a spell of making loaves of cranberry and banana bread and even fresh homemade bread to give away to friends or people in the neighborhood who were too poor to afford all these goodies.

In those days, money was not too plentiful so homemade cooking was a wonderful way to show the Christmas spirit. Yes, the week before Christmas was a busy one in our household and it seemed all the activity was around the kitchen stove. Oh, I forgot the divinity fudge and popcorn balls that Mother used to make for our stockings, long after we were tucked in bed. This way, she was sure she would have some left for Christmas Eve.

Gertrude Rudberg

Christmas Greetings

It's Christmastime; the church bells chime;
There's gladness everywhere;
Children sing and sleigh bells ring;
There's laughter in the air.

As carols are sung, and stockings hung,
We trim the Christmas tree;
Gifts are exchanged, and rearranged,
Midst happiness and glee.

As joy abounds, we hear the sounds
Of gladness, love, and cheer;
Be sure you send, to every friend,
Good wishes for the year.

On Christmas Morn, our Lord was born;
We celebrate his birth;
So, let us share a common prayer
For lasting peace on earth.

Billie McCoy

Christmastime

The sky is filled with twinkling stars,
The ground a snowy white,
And Christmas chimes ring solemnly
Across the wintry night.

Soft voices rise in caroling
The tidings of Christ's birth,
While warm and lovely thoughtfulness
Encompasses the earth.

Glad greetings wing across the land,
Small messengers of cheer,
To wish you Christmas happiness,
And a wonderful, bright New Year!

Fannie Newman

A Christmas Journey

It was neither the best of times nor the worst of times—it was Christmas Eve 1938. Looking out the train window with a nine-year-old wonderment at the vastness of the mountains, I was amazed at the curving train track stretching endlessly before me. The train was nearly empty, a phenomenon that later would be wondered at during the war years that loomed ahead. This was, however, 1938; and the war rumbles in Europe seemed remote to those of us from a small town in Minnesota. I peered into the darkness and felt strange and lonely. This should be the "best of times." My father, for the first time in his life, had received time off with pay and this was our first real vacation. The only bleak spot was we had to take it in December. Since we had relatives who would provide lodging, my parents decided we could afford a visit to the faraway state of Washington.

The thought of being away from home on Christmas had never entered my mind, and I am sure my parents thought the possibility unlikely. Nevertheless, here we were on our way west to Washington state. If we were still in Minnesota, I thought to myself, there would be grandparents, aunts, uncles, and cousins gathered for the holidays. The warmth of those family holidays were as much a part of Christmas as the well-worn creche, the blue snow that seemed to fall only on Christmas Eve, and the sound of sleigh bells. The crunch of the sleigh over the crisp dry snow and those tinkling sleigh bells were our last link to the gentle past of my grandparents.

The depression never seemed to dampen those early Christmases with the family gathered round. The table was always laden with the summer's harvest of fruit, vegetables, fish, and fowl: a smorgasbord prepared by the loving hands of my mother and grandmother. At Christmastime, my grandmother became a wizard with the needle and thread and amazing outfits were brought forth. Upon close inspection I could tell that the blue velvet had once been a long dress of my mother's from a better day, but it was still beautiful, if slightly large. Grandma always left room for me to grow, even after I stopped growing. My great-uncle was a miracle worker with saw and hammer; and from scraps of wood from his shop, he turned a little girl's wishes into realities of doll cradles and dressing tables, just nine-year-old size. My parents seemed to have a special communication with the jolly man in the red suit and white beard. Only much later, did I learn that a visit from Santa Claus came by way of my parents' hard-earned and diligently saved pennies.

The memories, like blue snow, were in Minnesota; and somehow the Rocky Mountains didn't look that great. What was so exciting about the Great Divide? The few people on the train seemed deep in their own thoughts; the three of us were quite alone. My grandmother had put up quite an argument about our leaving; however, my father with equal determination had said, "Ya, we are going."

Now all of us seemed to be having second thoughts; no one spoke as the train wound its way around the mountainside. Once in awhile one of the passengers would laugh rather harshly; and someone tried singing a Christmas carol, but the notes died as suddenly as they started. We had eaten our Christmas Eve dinner in the dining car, whose decorations seemed to mock the holiday. My grandmother had packed a basket of food big enough for a much larger family; but my dad felt it a special treat to eat with the other passengers. Even though I knew he couldn't afford the expense, it just wasn't the family smorgasbord. Typical kid, I started to pout.

Without saying a word, my mother reached into her large bag and pulled out a book. She put her arm around me and started to read, " . . . And it came to pass that in those days there went out a decree . . . " I had heard the story many times before, but never to the rhythmic click of train wheels and the swaying of the coach with its gloomy yellow lights, and the musty smell that seemed peculiar to trains.

Mother read about another family that, two thousand years ago, found themselves in a strange land. They, too, felt alone and were without a home. Although our "homeless" condition was temporary, I could empathize with that family of so long ago. A sudden warmth seemed to surround us. Then I realized that Christmas was not a place, house, or time; it was people being together and loving each other—like that First Family. I was nine, but I suddenly felt very grown-up and loved.

Dolores Johnson Heffelfinger

Christmas Snow

The world lay sleeping through the night
As snow fell silent, soft, and white.

It covered the grass so long turned brown,
It trimmed the trees with eiderdown;
It came to rest in the outstretched arm
Of the tall blue spruce, and snowflake charm
Changed the tarnished, the worn, the bare
To glistening beauty everywhere—
A promise of love, of a world apart,
A mantle from heaven to cover each heart.

We woke and found God's Christmas card
Painted in our own backyard.

Doris Brueggemann

How very nice when heaven sends
A Christmas pure and white,
With just enough of winter snow
To add a rich delight;
All tissue-wrapped in snowflakes, dear,
How lovely to believe,
We know there is no gift as grand
As snow on Christmas Eve.

What priceless treasure we behold
All silver in the dawn,
A world beneath new-fallen snow
Just as the dark is gone;
A silent holiness brings peace,
All earth a lovely sight,
God seems to touch the world with love
In snow on Christmas night.

Garnett Ann Schultz

LaVerne P. Larson

What inspires a tomboy, whose interest seems to lie solely in sports, to become a poet? Just ask LaVerne P. Larson. Born and bred in Chicago, Illinois, Miss Larson has enthusiastically participated in all kinds of outdoor sports, from baseball and tennis to biking and roller skating. Spending so much time outdoors has developed a love of nature and its changing seasons which inspired her poetry exalting the wonder and beauty of life. Her retirement from the Illinois Bell Telephone Company, after thirty years of service, allows Miss Larson more time to spend on her hobbies. Accompanied by her nine-year-old German schnauzer Tippy she enjoys photography, gardening, and corresponding with her friends. Writing poetry, however, still occupies the majority of her time: "My poems, like a garden in my heart, seem to grow with the passing years." And grow they do, enriching the lives of all who read them.

One Wish for Christmas

If I had one wish for Christmas
That really would come true,
I'd wish that Christmas joy and peace
Would last the whole year through.

Hearts are filled with joy and love,
Folks go to church and pray,
On the eve that brought our Savior
And on the morn of Christmas Day.

Songs and stories, old yet new,
Are told around the tree,
As it stands in splendid radiance
For everyone to see.

There is pleasure gained in giving
And a quiet, inner glow,
For in making someone happy
The angels sing, you know.

If I had one wish for Christmas
I know it would bring cheer,
If the folks on earth just carried
Christmas in their hearts all year.

Pototschnik

At Christmastime

Bless the whole wide world, dear God,
Upon this Christmas Day,
Let hope and faith, love and peace
Come to light the way.

Within the golden candle glow
The bells' sweet silver chime,
The stories and the carols sung,
Let all know Christmastime.

The shining radiant evergreen,
Each gift, and card, and prayer,
In glistening snow and twinkling star
It is Christmas, everywhere.

Let's Have Snow for Christmas

Oh, let's have snow for Christmas
Upon that special night,
When long ago one bright star
Shone its holy light.

The crystal flakes from heaven,
Falling from above,
Seem to hold a message
Of God's faith, and hope, and love.

Each one's a shining symbol
Enfolding city, farm, and town,
Like God's reverent benediction
In a shimmering, silver crown.

They bring a lovely silence
And hush the sounds of earth,
As though to make men everywhere
Know of our Savior's birth.

Oh, let's have snow for Christmas
To bring us trust and cheer
In Him who watches over us—
Every day and night all year.

Christmas

A most delightful time of year,
When everyone is of good cheer.
Love and hope and faith abound,
As merry hearts gather round.

The evergreen is trimmed so fine,
And twinkles with a look divine.
Holly and the mistletoe
Are hung wherever you may go.

Little children starry-eyed,
Dream of Santa's reindeer ride.
Carols echo through the air,
Like a sweet and reverent prayer.

And stories of the Christ Child's birth
Are told and cherished o'er the earth.
Snowflakes make a fairyland,
White and sparkling, oh, so grand.

And dinner is a special treat
When families gather round to eat.
The peace and love that Christmas brings
Forever comes on angel wings.

Be It Ever So Humble

Home is where the heart is . . . where love and reverence reign . . . where there is a spirit of harmony and a feeling of safe security . . . where there is neither selfishness, nor bickering, nor discord, nor a lack of respect . . . where the great virtues of sympathy, kindness, and gentleness are practiced every hour of every day . . . where the child learns to know, to understand, and to practice only that which is right . . . where we come together to find the joy and the happiness of the companionship of family and the fellowship of friends, and to say grace at mealtime and a prayer at close of day.

And at this Yuletide season let us be reminded that all this had its beginning with the birth of the Christ Child in the most humble of places. Just as that first humble Christian home radiated love, faith, hope, and charity, let us likewise carry these virtues in our hearts . . . but above all let us be humble and forgiving not just for an hour or a day, but for every day . . . then and only then shall there be "Peace on earth, good will among men."

Ethel G. Hokser

Christmas Eve

It's the eve before Christmas,
A magical time
Of carols and candles
And church bells that chime.

Thinking of Christmases
Now and to come,
Of holly, of ivy,
Of choirs and psalms.

Of doorbells and laughter,
Of families drawn nigh,
Of one shining star
In a frostbitten sky.

May we, like the wise men,
Still follow the star.
Seek after the vision
That beckons afar.

Kay Winters

Oh, What Fun
It Used to Be

Oh, what fun it used to be,
Carrying home the new-chopped tree.
Yuletide greetings, echoing around
Snowflakes falling gently down.

Shopping at the General Store,
Touching gifts, one moment more.
On the ice pond, skating fun,
Rosy cheeks on everyone.

Children at their very best
For Christmas Eve's final test.
Mom and Dad with haunting walk,
Ofttimes just a whispered talk.

Sleigh bells jingled in the night,
Glistening from a star so bright.
Laughter ringing from each mouth,
Joyful singing all about.

Popcorn balls on trees so tall,
Taffy apples from the fall.
Stockings on the chimney hung,
On the doorsteps caroling sung.

Snuggled close in quilted beds,
Wishful dreams in cherubs' heads,
From the Infant, newly born,
Blessings on this Christmas Morn.

Genevieve Klotz Palmas

Christmas Joy

The house is hung with cedar boughs,
    There's Christmas in the air,
The gifts are tied with tinsel bows
    And hidden everywhere.

Our days are filled with happiness,
    And all our hearts are merry;
We feel as gay and shining bright
    As any holly berry.

Our dearest friends trip in and out
    And greet the family.
A silver star is gleaming on
    The tip-top of the tree.

When blessed Christmastide is here,
    Our lives reflect its glow,
As joy of heaven kindles joy
    Upon the earth below.

Gail Brook Burket

Kindle the Hearth Fires

Kindle the hearth fires everywhere.
    Watch for the glowing light;
The light that will shower its warmth and cheer,
    This holy Christmas night.

Kindle the fires that never go out;
    See how the sparks are hurled.
They lighten the darkness in fields of gloom
    And warm the hearts of the world.

Kindle the fires that symbolize love;
    Light them in ways untrod.
They are the hope of the suffering earth;
    They are the paths of God.

Agnes Davenport Bond

Christmas Made Brighter

When it comes to Christmas tree ornaments—and it comes to them each and every year—the beautiful, reflective work of Wib Lauter adds a special home-made touch to the season. Wib Lauter is known as "the Tin Man of Wyomissing Hills, Pennsylvania." Not to be confused with the tin man, the straw man, and the timid lion of *The Wizard of Oz*, Wib is a wizard in his own right. He makes bright, glistening Christmas tree ornaments from tin—samples of which are shown on these pages.

Wib Lauter came upon the art of tinsmithing quite by accident. At one time, Wib (Wibbert) owned and operated a busy kitchen manufacturing and retailing business. On a visit to the Landis Valley Farm Museum in Lancaster County, Pennsylvania, a pierced tin lantern caught his eye. When he returned home, he read everything he could lay his hands on relative to the craft of tinsmithing, acquired some tin and antiquated tools, and reproduced his own tin lantern. Lauter became more and more interested in the art of tinsmithing, devoting his weekends and evenings to this hobby. When he sold his business in 1976, he had more time available and began making a collection of lamps and lanterns which he calls "The History of Lighting." Upon completion, he expects to have 200 fixtures in this collection, 110 of which are already finished.

It is his collection of Christmas tree ornaments, however, which are perhaps the most fanciful. In 1978 a report reached the Lauters that Mrs. Walter Mondale, long interested in the arts, had requested handcrafted ornaments for her Christmas tree be sent to the Museum of Modern Arts in New York City. Lauter submitted several which were accepted and adorned the Vice-President's Christmas tree.

Lauter begins his construction of the ornaments with a large sheet of tin which he cuts into 3 x 3½-inch circles or squares. To form the designs he uses tools which are a composite of tools from many trades and professions, such as crimpers, shears and nibblers from the sheet metal trade, notchers from the metalworking trade, hemostadts from the medical profession and improvised pliers with rollers on the end which Lauter himself created. For ideas, Web's wife and daughter contribute their imaginations; so the Lauter family together arrive at new and distinctive designs. At present, they have approximately twenty basic designs, including a tin angel, a Pennsylvania Dutch heart, a poinsettia, and a large star for the top of the tree.

Wib Lauter's tin art has been shown at countless festivals and fine arts displays. The creations of "The Tin Man" are so intriguing to all who see them that Wib has become quite popular as a lecturer and leader of workshops where he helps others try their hand at making their own ornaments. His rewarding and fascinating hobby of ten years has turned into a life's work; and, in the process brings joy to others. Wherever it appears, the collection of tin ornaments and lanterns catches viewers' eyes—and their fancies as well.

Gale Brennan

The Yuletide
Is a Joyous Time

The Yuletide is a joyous time
   for hearthstone flaming bright,
And carolers of happy voice
   laud gaily through the night.

The candlelight in windows tells
   of tidings that abound,
Where warmth and mirth—Goodwill on earth
   may surely there be found.

And snow-crowned landscapes stretching forth
   against the pewter sky
Add harmony and glowing warmth
   to curious passersby.

The Yuletide is a precious time,
   like fragrance of old lace,
For riches rare, nor glittered gold,
   can this great wealth replace.

Jessie Bell

A Legend from the Hills

There's a beautiful Christmas fable
That is told when the bright star appears,
Of a boy, a lamb, and a stable;
I have cherished it all through the years.

A boy stood high on a mountainous spot,
On a bright, cold winter's eve.
The wind, like spray from a fountain's top,
Whipped through his ragged sleeve.

He didn't feel his hands grow cold
For he had a mission to fill;
A lamb had strayed from the neighbor's fold,
And the neighbor was worried and ill.

The boy called out, though no sound came
But the crunch of his feet in the snow.
He searched every place, called again and again.
There was no place left he could go.

Then he rubbed his hands to get them warm
And raised his tear-dimmed eyes.
He saw the lamb huddled safe from harm
By the light of a star in the skies.

"Oh, you poor little lamb," the little boy cried.
"Let me hold you and make you warm."
And he carried it down the mountainside
Till he brought it home safe from harm.

The star that had shone on the mountaintop
Followed close in a stardust fall.
It passed fine churches and houses to stop
Near the lamb as it lay in the stall.

The boy grew warm as the star shone bright
For the lamb stood up on its feet.
The stable glowed with a heavenly light,
And a voice came, soft and sweet.

"You have learned what the meaning of love is.
It will bless you wherever you are.
In your heart it will always be Christmas
For Love is the Bethlehem Star."

Alice Leedy Mason

And There Were Shepherds

In the grass-covered hills of Judea,
Shepherds, watching their flocks by night,
Heard the sound of heavenly music
And their awe-stricken hearts filled with fright.

The glory of God shone about them
While the wonderful story was told,
"Born to you in the city of David
Is the Christ who was promised of old.

"This is the sign given to you—
A manger will be His bed."
Then a chorus of heavenly voices
In praise of the Savior said,

"All glory to God in the highest
And peace be on earth among men!"
Like a dream, angels came and vanished.
Shepherds listened amazed at the scene.

From the grass-covered hills of Judea
They hastened to find where He lay.
Angels brought them a special message
And a star would show them the way.

Brenda Leigh

The Christmas Story

And it came to pass in those days, that there went out a decree from Caesar Augustus, that all the world should be taxed. (And this taxing was first made when Cyrenius was governor of Syria.) And all went to be taxed, every one into his own city. And Joseph also went up from Galilee, out of the city of Nazareth, into Judaea, unto the city of David, which is called Bethlehem; (because he was of the house and lineage of David:) To be taxed with Mary his espoused wife, being great with child. And so it was, that, while they were there, the days were accomplished that she should be delivered. And she brought forth her firstborn son, and wrapped him in swaddling clothes, and laid him in a manger; because there was no room for them in the inn. And there were in the same country shepherds abiding in the field, keeping watch over their flock by night. And, lo, the angel of the Lord came upon them, and the glory of the Lord shone round about them: and they were sore afraid. And the angel said unto them, *Fear not: for, behold, I bring you good tidings of great joy, which shall be to all people. For unto you is born this day in the city of David a Savior, which is Christ the Lord. And this shall be a sign unto you; Ye shall find the babe wrapped in swaddling clothes, lying in a manger.* And suddenly there was with the angel a multitude of the heavenly host praising God, and saying, *Glory to God in the highest, and on earth peace, good will toward men.* And it came to pass, as the angels were gone away from them into heaven, the shepherds said one to another. *Let us now go even unto Bethlehem, and see this thing which is come to pass, which the Lord hath made known unto us.* And they came with haste, and found Mary, and Joseph, and the babe lying in a manger. And when they had seen it, they made known abroad the saying which was told them concerning this child. And all they that heard it wondered at those things which were told them by the shepherds. But Mary kept all these things and pondered them in her heart. And the shepherds returned, glorifying and praising God for all the things that they had heard and seen, as it was told unto them.

Luke 2:1-20

Handel's Christmas Masterpiece

The aging composer, bowed by misfortune, wandered the lonely streets of London nightly in hopeless despair. Only memories of his past glory, when the brilliant man was touted by the court society of London and Europe, were left to him and it now seemed his musical genius was gone forever. George Frederick Handel, once the favorite of kings and queens, had been forced into bankruptcy and had become a pauper.

One bitterly cold morning during the winter of 1741 Handel returned to his lodgings to find a thick package on the table. It contained a text made up of scripture verses from the librettist, Charles Jennens. Dazed by cold and hunger, Handel listlessly leafed through the pages.

Comfort ye, comfort ye, My people, saith your God . . . Behold! A virgin shall conceive and bear a Son, and shall call His name Emmanuel, God with us . . . The people that walked in darkness have seen a great light . . . For unto us a Child is born, unto us a Son is given . . . and His name shall be called Wonderful Counsellor, The Mighty God . . . Then shall the eyes of the blind be opened, and the ears of the deaf unstopped . . . He shall feed His flock like a shepherd: and He shall gather the lambs with His arm, and carry them in His bosom . . . .

Excitedly, he read on. "He was despised and rejected of men; a man of sorrows and acquainted with grief . . . He looked for some to have pity on Him, but there was no man; neither found He any to comfort Him . . . But thou didst not leave His soul in hell . . . ."

He hurriedly read on. "I know that my Redeemer liveth, and that He shall stand at the latter day upon the earth . . . King of Kings, and Lord of Lords, Hallelujah!"

The words burned into his soul and struck a responsive chord within him. He rushed to the piano with pencil in hand and began to write the music to the immortal *Messiah*. For two weeks he labored incessantly.

Handel saw no one and refused food and sleep. At last he finished the great oratorio and a friend was admitted to his room. Tears were streaming down his face. "I did think I did see all Heaven before me, and the great God Himself," he declared at the completion of the glorious "Hallelujah Chorus."

The composition was first heard in Dublin where it was an overwhelming triumph. Several weeks later it was again a tumultuous success in London. During this performance the King, carried away by the glory of the great "Hallelujah Chorus," rose to his feet and the audience followed his example! Today, audiences all over the world still rise and remain standing during this Chorus.

In succeeding years, George Frederick Handel became blind, ill and poor. But the composer of the great masterpiece never again permitted his misfortunes to overcome his spirit.

One evening in April, at the age of seventy-four, Handel collapsed during a performance of the *Messiah*.

Handel went to be with his heavenly Father forever on April 13, 1759.

Marie King

Journey through Many Christmases

"Over there," said the tall young Israeli cameraman Rolf Kneller, "is the town of Bethlehem." Cloaked in purplish mist, the parapets and buildings of the ancient city where Jesus was born were clearly discernible. As I looked across the valleys and hills toward that hallowed place, it seemed that for the first time in my life the Bible had become comprehensible. Seeing that countryside through which the shepherds once followed the star to the manger where Jesus was born, I felt the reality and the meaning of that holy story more fully than I had ever felt them before.

We were standing on one of the hilliest points of Jerusalem. To our left we could see Old Jerusalem, which was given to the Arabs when the armistice was signed, and on the buildings around us we could see the battle scars that remained from the bitter fight between Arabs and Israelis.

The day before, in Rome, Bob Weitman and attended Mass at St. Susanna Church. We had gone there not only because I knew the pastor Paulist Father Cunningham, but also because that church is the burial place of St. Genesius the patron saint of entertainers. When we heard the Gospel, which that day told of Jesus going down to Jerusalem, I whispered to Bob "It seems incredible that we'll be there tomorrow."

Now we were actually in Jerusalem and already becoming steeped in biblical lore.

We had traveled by car from Tel Aviv to Jerusalem over the same roads that the Israeli Army a short time before had used in fighting their way to relieve the beleaguered city. When we started climbing I realized for the first time that Jerusalem was in the mountains. As we neared the city we noticed the heights of Jordan towering above us on the left.

"Up there," our driver said, "the Jordanians had their heavy guns, and they were able to wipe our convoys off the road. We couldn't get anything through. Then some of our biblical scholars went to the Army chiefs and told them that in the days of Jesus there was another road into Jerusalem. The Army engineers investigated and found the Bible was right. They brought up their bulldozers at night and dug out the ancient road on the sheltered side of the mountain, and the troops were able to make their way into Jerusalem."

It is inspiring to learn that the extensive excavations now being carried on in Israel are constantly producing new confirmation of events that are recorded in the Bible. Even non-believers are overwhelmed by the massive evidence that is being uncovered by the archaeologists. In Israel, youngsters start learning the Bible from the first day they go to school; people discuss biblical events as naturally as we discuss baseball and the weather. A visitor soon finds himself thinking and talking in the same vein. During my stay it seemed that every radio set in Israel was tuned in on an international quiz show on the Bible, ultimately won by an Israeli. When we were leaving the country, our driver gave us each a present—a Bible.

Standing on that height in Jerusalem and looking toward Bethlehem in the purplish distance, I thought of the Gospel according to St. Luke, and a fresh feeling of understanding swept over me.

"It happened that a decree went out at this time from the Emperor Augustus, enjoining that the whole world should be registered; this register was the first one made during the time when Cyrinus was Governor of Syria. All must go and give in their names, each in his own city; and Joseph, being of David's clan and family, came up from the town of Nazareth, in Galilee, to David's city in Judaea, the city called Bethlehem, to give in his name there. With him was his espoused wife Mary, who was then in her pregnancy; and it was while they were still there that the time came for her delivery. She brought forth a son, her first-born, whom she wrapped in his swaddling-clothes, and laid in a manger, because there was no room for them in the inn."

Looking out over that holy ground, I could easily picture Joseph and Mary coming down from the hills and taking their twelve-year-old son to Jerusalem for the feast of the Passover. I could imagine the consternation of Joseph and Mary on discovering the child was lost and their amazement when they found him in the Temple "sitting in the midst of the doctors and asking them questions. And all that heard him were astonished at his understanding and answers."

Time and again I've thought back to that moving experience of mine in Jerusalem and have tried to visualize the drama of the Nativity that took place in the little town of Bethlehem. For the Nativity scene is a part of my heritage, and picturing it never fails to take me back to early fondly remembered Christmases.

All seven of us—Mother, Father, and five kids—would attend the Solemn High Mass on Christmas Eve. In our church at Port Chester, New York, I remember Father John Waters and Father Hugh Gilmartin chanting from the altar, the choir responding, the beauty and mystery and pageantry of the service. But even more clearly I recall the little Nativity scene constructed before the statue of the Virgin Mary, the miniature animals pressing forward curiously to see the Babe in swaddling clothes lying on the straw.

I was a boy of five when we moved from East Harlem to Port Chester. There, in the country, there was nothing strange about the idea of this birth in a stable. Our priest, Father Fitzsimmons, and our family doctor, Edward Quinlan, each rode around in a buggy behind a horse. I knew the Burns Livery Stable well. I knew the curiosity of animals, I knew the softness of a bed of straw. . . . So many wonderful Christmas Eves I had heard the thrilling words from the pulpit, "And it came to pass in those days. . . ."

Ed Sullivan

CHRISTMAS WITH ED SULLIVAN by Ed Sullivan. From CHRISTMAS WITH ED SULLIVAN, Copyright © 1959 by Ed Sullivan, McGraw-Hill Publishers. Used with permission.

The Innkeeper's Son
A Christmas Story

Brian F. King

It was the time of the taking of the census in Bethlehem of Judea. The narrow streets of the ancient little town teemed with traffic of every possible description as subjects of the Roman Empire came from every direction to register their names and those of their families with scribes who sat at little tables in the marketplace. Never had Bethlehem known such a busy time! Camels—their harness bells ringing merrily in the cold stillness of early evening—jostled each other as they wended their way through the crowded streets. Seemingly endless processions of donkeys—some carrying as many as four children on their backs—plodded patiently along cobble-stoned lanes, breathing little bouquets of frost flowers into the lavender veil of dusk. Tall centurions, their bronze armor glistening in the waning light of sunset, forced their way through the hubbub and confusion, occasionally using the flat sides of their short swords to drive loiterers out of their path.

There was no room for guests in the inns of Bethlehem in the time of which we write. All available lodgings had been contracted for earlier in the day, and families arriving in the town at the time of twilight discovered to their dismay that shelter of any kind simply wasn't to be had. Resignedly they pitched makeshift tents beneath the sheltering cliffs of rocky hillsides, or huddled beneath blankets in the marketplace to wait out the passage of the long hours of a cold night.

Mark, the seven-year-old son of the keeper of a tiny inn on the outskirts of Bethlehem, watched the arrival of the endless stream of camel caravans, donkey trains and foot-weary people with keen interest. He was fascinated by the tinkling music of the camels' bells and the colorful robes of the people. It was an exciting experience for the small boy and he enjoyed the sights and sounds created by the restless multitudes of travelers as they knocked vainly at the doors of inns and hostelries in search of lodgings for the night.

Despite his delight in the largest visitation of people to Bethlehem that he had ever witnessed, Mark didn't relish the task that had been assigned to him—that of standing at the doorway of his father's inn and informing travelers that there was no room for them. It hurt the small boy to see the looks of disappointment on the faces of the travelers he was forced to turn away, and he felt the deepest sympathy for them.

Mark had been standing vigil at his disagreeable task since midday and he was still at his post as darkness began to settle over the distant hills. Hungry and weary, he leaned on the crutches that supported his withered legs and wistfully wished that he could run and play like other children. But he knew in his heart that such a miracle would never come to pass, for physicians had told him—when his legs had been robbed of their strength by a mysterious illness when he was five years old—that he would never walk without crutches.

It was close to the hour of eleven before the flow of humanity began to dwindle from the streets.

"It will be good to enjoy a bowl of broth and a warm bed," Mark thought longingly as travelers began to slowly disappear from the streets. A few moments later, the last weary traveler had vanished in the distance and—his weary vigil at an end—Mark headed for the cheery warmth of the inn's kitchen.

The small boy had hobbled only a few steps toward his destination when he was hailed by a firm but gentle voice that emanated from the dark mouth of a narrow side street. Peering through the dim haze of starlight, Mark saw a tall, bearded man leading a donkey on which rode a heavily veiled lady.

"Have you room at the inn?" the bearded stranger inquired, approaching the youngster.

"I'm sorry, but there isn't a room to be had," Mark apologized. "Some of our guests are even sleeping on the floor."

"We have come a long way and my spouse is weary to the point of illness," the bearded stranger said. "Shelter of any kind would be most welcome."

"I wish I could help you, but I can't," Mark replied. Then, bracing himself on his crutches, he began to hobble away.

Mark hadn't taken more than a few steps, however, when a wave of compassion for the bearded stranger and his lady all but overwhelmed him. Turning to face them he said, "There is no room at the inn, as I've explained, but if you wouldn't mind sleeping in the stable, perhaps I could find some straw for your beds and make you comfortable."

"Anything at all will do," the bearded man said. Then he added, "I am Joseph and this is my wife, Mary."

Mark led the travelers to the inn's stable. There he showed them where to find straw for their beds. Then he hobbled off to the inn to find blankets for them.

It took Mark a considerable period of time to locate blankets for his guests. When he returned to the stable with them, he discovered that a third guest—a tiny Infant—lay in the arms of the wife of the bearded stranger.

"This is my newborn Son, Jesus," Mary explained.

"We must find a bed for the Child!" Mark exclaimed in deep concern. "Such a tiny Infant will catch cold without a warm bed on a wintry night like this!" And, hobbling as fast as he could, he gathered odd pieces of wood and fashioned them into a crude crib, which he filled with hay.

Mary placed the Infant in the crib and smiled at Mark.

"May God bless you for your gentle heart," she said to the small boy. And Mark blushed in embarrassment.

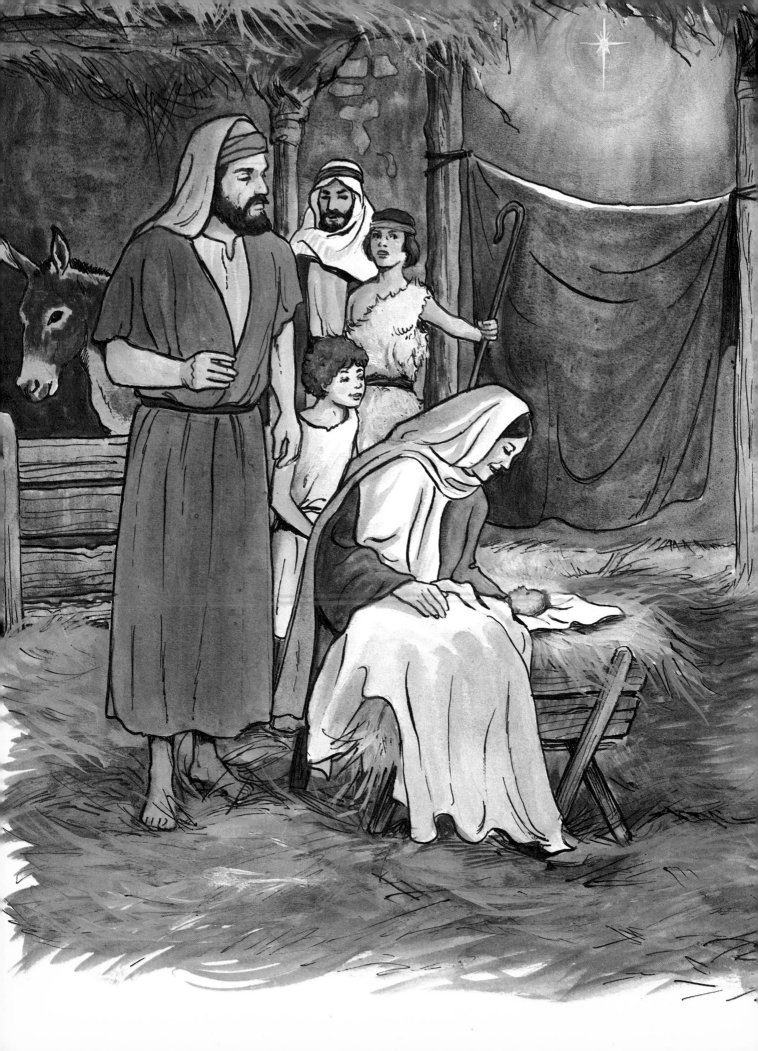

A few moments later, all sorts of strange and wonderful things began to take place in the humble stable. Three great kings from the East, their robes sparkling with jewels and rich brocades, entered and laid precious gifts at the feet of the Christ Child. Shepherds came to kneel and pray and—venturing out into the wintry night—Mark saw that a great silver star shone in the heavens directly overhead. The small boy was awed by all of these things and his heart was suddenly filled with gladness.

"Who is this Child that kings come to worship Him?" he asked one of the shepherds. "He is the Savior of the world. He is the Son of God," the man replied. And Mark somehow knew the shepherd spoke the truth.

Reentering the stable, Mark stood before the Infant and bowed his head in prayer. "I have no gifts, such as the gold, frankincense, and myrrh that the great kings from the East brought You. All I have to give You is the humble crib in which You lie," he whispered to the Infant. The Baby smiled and placed a tiny hand on Mark's forehead. Mark kissed the chubby little fingers and then reverently took his leave of the Child. He was well outside the stable door when he suddenly realized that he had left his crutches behind him. And, when he looked down at his legs, he was astonished to find that they were healed.

Tears of thankfulness streamed down the small boy's face as he stood in the blinding white light of the great silver star of Bethlehem. And, as he gave silent thanks for the miracle that had been bestowed on him, a voice spoke from out of the stillness of the night, saying: "Your health has been restored. It is the gift of the Christ Child in return for your gift of the crib in which He lies. Yours is a gift of love indeed!" And from that day forth Mark's days were endowed with health and happiness.

In later years Mark became the most celebrated cabinetmaker in the East. Specimens of his work adorned the palaces of kings and princes. But his most cherished work of all was the crude crib he had—as a small boy—fashioned for the Christ Child. Covered with a cloth of gold, it occupied the place of honor in his home for the remainder of his days. Such is the story of the son of an innkeeper of Bethlehem who lived long, long ago.

LIGHT A CANDLE

When the Christmas season passes,
　With its mistletoe and pine,
Keep your candle in the window
　So its guiding light will shine
Just as bright on each tomorrow
　As it did on Christmas Day.
Keep within your heart the spirit
　That is Christmas charity.

Christmas glitter soon grows tarnished,
　But one candle in the night
Offers guidance to the wanderer
　Looking for a beacon light.
It will shine in honest welcome
　For the stranger who will see
Friendly welcome in a town that
　Otherwise might lonely be.

So just put away your presents,
　Take the trimmings from your tree,
But don't lock away the spirit
　That is Christmas charity.
Light a candle in your window,
　Never let it fade away . . .
Keep it just as bright tomorrow
　As it was on Christmas Day!

Helen Williams

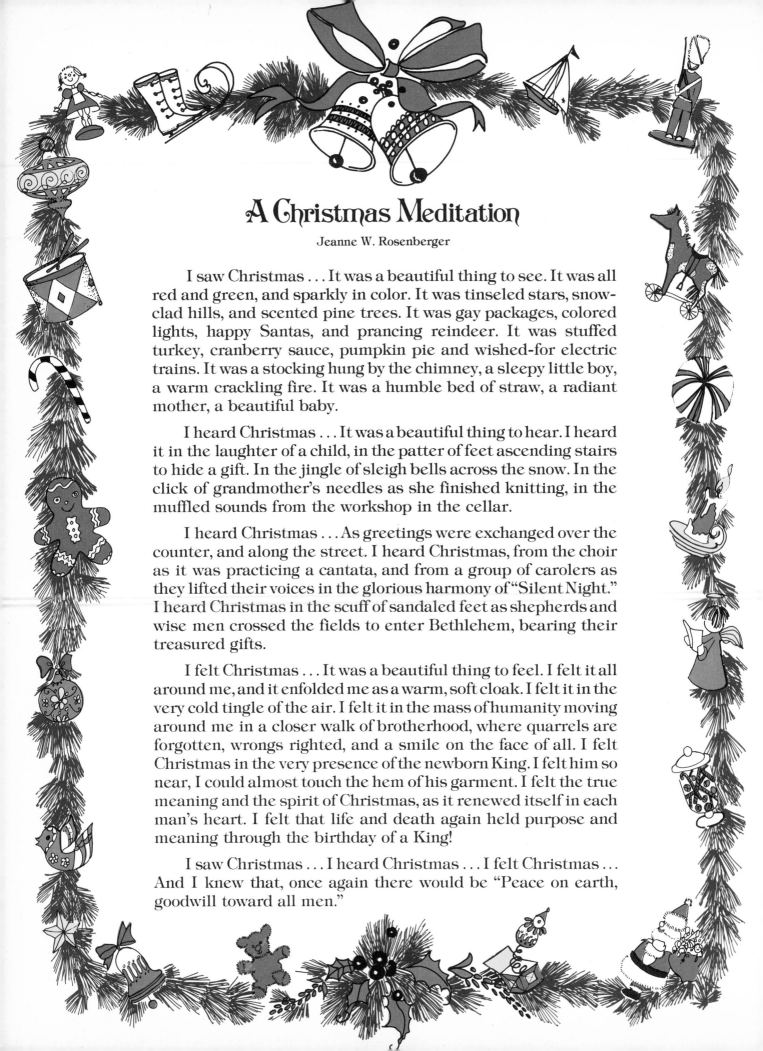

A Christmas Meditation

Jeanne W. Rosenberger

I saw Christmas . . . It was a beautiful thing to see. It was all red and green, and sparkly in color. It was tinseled stars, snow-clad hills, and scented pine trees. It was gay packages, colored lights, happy Santas, and prancing reindeer. It was stuffed turkey, cranberry sauce, pumpkin pie and wished-for electric trains. It was a stocking hung by the chimney, a sleepy little boy, a warm crackling fire. It was a humble bed of straw, a radiant mother, a beautiful baby.

I heard Christmas . . . It was a beautiful thing to hear. I heard it in the laughter of a child, in the patter of feet ascending stairs to hide a gift. In the jingle of sleigh bells across the snow. In the click of grandmother's needles as she finished knitting, in the muffled sounds from the workshop in the cellar.

I heard Christmas . . . As greetings were exchanged over the counter, and along the street. I heard Christmas, from the choir as it was practicing a cantata, and from a group of carolers as they lifted their voices in the glorious harmony of "Silent Night." I heard Christmas in the scuff of sandaled feet as shepherds and wise men crossed the fields to enter Bethlehem, bearing their treasured gifts.

I felt Christmas . . . It was a beautiful thing to feel. I felt it all around me, and it enfolded me as a warm, soft cloak. I felt it in the very cold tingle of the air. I felt it in the mass of humanity moving around me in a closer walk of brotherhood, where quarrels are forgotten, wrongs righted, and a smile on the face of all. I felt Christmas in the very presence of the newborn King. I felt him so near, I could almost touch the hem of his garment. I felt the true meaning and the spirit of Christmas, as it renewed itself in each man's heart. I felt that life and death again held purpose and meaning through the birthday of a King!

I saw Christmas . . . I heard Christmas . . . I felt Christmas . . . And I knew that, once again there would be "Peace on earth, goodwill toward all men."

Holiday Wishes

I wish you the best for Christmas,
And for the coming year,
It seems like such a short time
Since last Christmas was here.

Remember when we were children
And the time so slowly came,
For all the Christmas good things,
And songs of the Christ Child's name?

But since it's another Christmas,
We will do as we have before,
And be just as busy with
All the holidays have in store.

I will take time out for your greetings
Just to wish all my dear ones the best,
And may Jesus, the author of Christmas,
Be with you each one to bless.

Lou Celia Kuehner

Christmas Joy

Christmastime is full of joy,
For every little girl and boy;
For Mom and Dad and cousins, too,
There is no time for feeling blue.
The Christmas tree is set in place
And trimmed with all the pomp and grace,
With tinsel bright and colored balls,
That sparkle when the tree light falls
Upon this colorful array
That helps to brighten up our day.
The stockings, filled by Santa's elves,
Are hung upon the fireplace shelves,
And all the toys beneath the tree
Shine brightly now for you and me.

Lucille Leedy Swales

The Toy Maker

Donald R. Stoltz

Once upon a time in a little toy shop, there worked a very poor toy maker. Although he was the best toy maker for miles around, he hardly made enough money to feed his wife and three children, for he had to pay a large amount of money each month in rent to the manager of the building, Mr. Grausam. And as the poor toy maker made more toys and more money, the rent went up and up. In order to feed and clothe his family, he also had to make toys at home, often working late into the night. Some nights he didn't even sleep at all.

One day about a week before Christmas, he was very busy in the toy shop trying to keep up with the holiday rush when the chime above the shop door rang. In walked a very stately gentleman with a black beard. "Good morning," said the toy maker. "Welcome to my shop. How may I help you?"

"Good morning, Heinz," said the gentleman. "I would like to order one hundred toy dancers and one hundred wooden soldiers for Christmas."

"Two hundred toys!" exclaimed the toy maker, his eyes opening wide, "two hundred toys in a week? Impossible! That would take me more than a month and I'm behind in my work as it is. Impossible!"

"Too bad, Heinz," said the man softly, "I could pay you one dollar a toy. Are you sure you can't do it?"

The toy maker whispered, "Two hundred dollars—I have never seen that much money! But I just can't do it. I'd probably have to give it all to Mr. Grausam for rent, anyway. He usually raises the rent this time of the year."

"Well, Heinz, think about it. I'll be back in a few days," said the bearded man as he started for the door.

"Wait a moment," called the toy maker. "One question before you go. Everyone in town calls me Mr. Toyman. No one even knows my first name. Where did you hear it? How did you know?"

Smiling, the man opened the door and left, saying, "I'll see you in three days, Heinz."

For the next few days, the toy maker worked very hard day and night making all kinds of Christmas toys. When he was finished, he started working on the two hundred soldiers and dancers for the strange gentleman. As he worked, he whistled and daydreamed of his family and the things he could buy them with two hundred dollars. Hour after hour he sat at his workbench and hammered and sawed and painted. Soon day turned into night, and as the hands on the cuckoo clock turned around, the toy maker could keep his eyes open no longer. In three days he had only finished twenty dancers and thirty soldiers; but he fell sound asleep.

"Good morning, Heinz!" a sharp voice called as the bell above the door chimed. The toy maker jumped to his feet, rubbing his eyes in the bright sunlight. "Ahah," said the gentleman, "I knew you could do it. One hundred soldiers and one hundred dancers, all finished. You're a good man, Heinz."

"But . . . but . . ." the toy maker stammered, "I didn't, I couldn't. I don't understand. . . ."

"Here you are, Heinz. Two hundred dollars as I promised."

At that very moment the shop door opened again, and in walked Mr. Grausam. "Well, Toyman, it looks like you're doing very well from all the money in your hand. That should just about cover this month's rent."

"But, Mr. Grausam, I have no money left for my family for Christmas," pleaded the toy man.

"Very well," sneered Mr. Grausam. "Here is ten dollars. Happy holiday, Toyman."

"Thank you," whispered the toy man as Mr. Grausam opened the door to go.

Suddenly the strange gentleman, who was quietly admiring the toys, turned, and in a loud, sharp voice cracked. "One moment, Mr. Grausam." Recognizing the voice of the stranger, Mr. Grausam turned.

"Mr. Gutman," he said meekly, "What are you doing here? Here is some of the money I owe you," he stammered, as he handed Mr. Gutman the money the toymaker had given him.

"Give the money to Mr. Toyman, Grausam. You are no longer the manager," said the gentleman. "I'm knocking this building down. I have better things to do with my land. Good day, Mr. Grausam."

As Mr. Grausam left the toy shop, the toy maker said, with a tear in his eye, "Mr. Gutman, I appreciate the money, but if you destroy the building I will have no toy shop."

"You are correct, Heinz, but do not worry. I have big plans for you," smiled the gentleman. "Sit down, Heinz. I have something to tell you. My name is Jacob Gutman. Many, many years ago, when we were children, you were my closest friend. Oh, you would never recognize me with this beard. One day I became very sick, I was not expected to live. There was nothing the

THE TOYMAKER by Norman Rockwell

doctors could do. But that afternoon you came to visit me, and in your hands were a beautiful toy soldier and a toy dancer that you carved and painted just for me. I was so excited I jumped out of bed! When my parents and the doctor came in, they couldn't believe their eyes. You probably don't remember this for you were always so kind and generous, but I will never forget it. Soon after, I got better and returned to school. I vowed that someday I would return the favor. Since that time," Mr. Gutman continued, "I have become one of the largest toy manufacturers in the world. Now I plan to knock down this old building and build a huge toy factory. Will you, Heinz, be the president of my company?"

With large tears rolling down his cheeks, the toy maker could hardly express his gratitude. Mr. Gutman started to leave. "Oh, by the way, Heinz, I hope you didn't mind a little help last night. I knew you couldn't make all those toys I needed for the local hospital party, so I had some of my employees come over after you were asleep to give you some assistance. I even made one soldier and one dancer myself. Now we're even. My debt is repaid! Merry Christmas, Heinz."

Dr. Donald R. Stoltz
Pres. Norman Rockwell Museum
Phila. Pa.

The Message of Christmas

Christmas is snow all sparkling and bright
Wrapping the earth in a mantle of white,
Evergreen trees in feathery down,
And garlands of lights through the streets of the town.

Christmas is boughs of cedar and pine,
Tinsel and stars that twinkle and shine,
Candles aglow with flickering light
And church bells that ring in the still of the night.

Christmas is home, be it city or farm,
And hearth fires glowing so friendly and warm;
With friends gathered round, their voices so gay,
To wish one and all a glad Christmas Day.

Christmas is children with bright dancing eyes,
Waiting for Santa to come through the skies;
Ice skates, and drums, and striped candy canes,
Baby dolls, Teddy bears, puzzles, and games.

Christmas is greeting cards sent far and near,
Filling each heart with a message of cheer.
Christmas is songs that the carolers sing;
On the crisp air their sweet voices ring.

Christmas is shepherds out on a hill;
Hark to the tidings of peace and goodwill!
Christmas is worship, oh, hear the bells ring!
Come let us adore Him, Our Savior and King.

Marion Olson

The Magic
of Christmas

The magic of Christmas is so many things . . .
A wreath on the door, and a church bell that rings;

A kitchen that's bubbling with sugar and spice;
Red stockings o'erflowing with everything nice.

The magic of Christmas is seen everywhere . . .
A star on the tree, and a candle aflare;

A log on the fire with a flickering glow;
Streets that are blanketed with shimmering snow.

The magic of Christmas is felt in one's heart;
A Babe in a manger and shepherds apart.

A star of gold in the sky above;
The peace that is ours by showing love.

The magic of Christmas is so many things . . .
A tree in the window and carolers that sing;

A house filled with children bubbling over with cheer,
Anxiously awaiting St. Nick to appear.

The magic of Christmas is happiness and joy,
Wrapped up in the face of a small girl and boy

As they race down the stairway in eagerness and glee,
To scan all the toys neath the glittering tree.

Ruth H. Underhill

The Birds' Christmas Carol

Abridged version

Kate Douglas Wiggin

It was very early Christmas morning, and in the stillness of the dawn, with the soft snow falling on the housetops, a little child was born in the Bird household.

They had intended to name the baby Lucy if it were a girl; but they had not expected her on Christmas morning, and a real Christmas baby was not to be lightly named—the whole family agreed in that. . . .

Mrs. Bird lay in her room, weak, but safe and happy, with her sweet girl baby by her side and the heaven of motherhood opening again before her. Nurse was making gruel in the kitchen, and the room was dim and quiet. . . .

Suddenly a sound of music poured out into the bright air and drifted into the chamber. It was the boy choir singing Christmas anthems. . . . .

Carol, brothers, carol,
Carol joyfully,
Carol the good tidings,
Carol merrily!

The voices were brimming over with joy.

"Why, my baby," whispered Mrs. Bird in soft surprise, "I had forgotten what day it was. You are a little Christmas child, and we will name you 'Carol'—mother's Christmas Carol!". . . .

Perhaps because she was born in holiday time, Carol was a very happy baby. Of course, she was too tiny to understand the joy of Christmastide, but people say there is everything in a good beginning, and she may have breathed in unconsciously the fragrance of ever-greens and holiday dinners; while the peals of sleigh bells and the laughter of happy children may have fallen upon her baby ears and wakened in them a glad surprise at the merry world she had come to live in. . . .

It was December, ten years later.

Carol had seen nine Christmas trees lighted on her birthdays one after another; nine times she had assisted in the holiday festivities of the household, though in her babyhood her share of the gayeties was somewhat limited.

For five years, certainly, she had hidden presents for Mamma and Papa in their own bureau drawers. . . .

For five years she had heard "'Twas the night before Christmas," and hung up a scarlet stocking many sizes too big for her, and pinned a sprig of holly on her little white nightgown, to show Santa Claus that she was a "truly" Christmas child. . . .

But Christmas in the Birds' Nest was scarcely as merry now as it used to be in the bygone years, for the little child, that once brought such an added blessing to the day, lay month after month a patient, helpless invalid, in the room where she was born. She had never been very strong in body, and it was with a pang of terror her mother and father noticed, soon after she was five years old, that she began to limp, ever so slightly; to complain too often of weariness, and to nestle close to her mother, saying she "would rather not go out to play, please." The illness was slight at first, and hope was always stirring in Mrs. Bird's heart. . . .

A famous physician had visited them that day, and told them that some time, it might be in one year, it might be in more, Carol would slip quietly off into heaven, whence she came. . . .

Carol herself knew nothing of motherly tears and fatherly anxieties; she lived on peacefully in the room where she was born.

But you never would have known that room; for Mr. Bird had a great deal of money, and though he felt sometimes as if he wanted to throw it all in the sea, since it could not buy a strong body for his little girl, yet he was glad to make the place she lived in just as beautiful as it could be. . . .

Love-birds and canaries hung in their golden houses in the windows, and they, poor caged things, could hop as far from their wooden perches as Carol could venture from her little white bed.

On one side of the room was a bookcase filled with hundreds—yes, I mean it—with hundreds and hundreds of books; books with gay-colored pictures, books without; books with black and white outline sketches, books with none at all; books with verses, books with stories; books that made children laugh, and some, only a few, that made them cry; books with words of one syllable for tiny boys and girls, and books with words of fearful length to puzzle wise ones.

This was Carol's "Circulating Library." Every Saturday she chose ten books, jotting their names down in a diary; into these she slipped cards that said:

Please keep this book two weeks and read it.
With love
Carol Bird

Then Mrs. Bird stepped into her carriage and took the ten books to the Children's Hospital, and brought home ten others that she had left there the fortnight before.

This was a source of great happiness; for some of the Hospital children that were old enough to print or write, and were strong enough to do it, wrote Carol sweet little letters about the books, and she answered them, and they grew to be friends. (It is very funny, but you do not always have to see people to love them. Just think about it, and tell me if it isn't so.) . . .

On these particular December days she was happier than usual, for Uncle Jack was coming from England to spend the holidays. Dear, funny, jolly, loving, wise Uncle Jack, who came every two or three years, and brought so much joy with him that the world looked as black as a thundercloud for a week after he went away again. . . "I want to tell you all about my plans for Christmas this year, Uncle Jack," said Carol, on the first evening of his visit, "because it will be the loveliest one I ever had. The boys laugh at me for caring so much about it; but it isn't altogether because it is Christmas, nor because it is my birthday; but long, long ago, when I first began to be ill, I used to think, the first thing when I waked on Christmas morning, 'Today is Christ's birthday—'and mine!' I did not put the words close together, you know, because that made it seem too bold; but I first said, 'Christ's birthday,' out loud, and then, in a minute, softly to myself—and mine!' And so I do not quite feel about Christmas as other girls do. Mamma says she supposes that ever so many other children have been born on that day. I often wonder where they are, Uncle Jack, and whether it is a dear thought to them, too, or whether I am so much in bed, and so often alone, that it means more to me. Oh, I do hope that none of them are poor, or cold, or hungry; and I wish—I wish they were all as happy as I, because they are really my little brothers and sisters. Now, Uncle Jack, dear, I am going to try and make somebody happy every single Christmas that I live, and this year it is to be the 'Ruggleses in the rear'."

"That large and interesting brood of children in the little house at the end of the back garden?"

"Yes; isn't it nice to see so many together? And, Uncle Jack, why do the big families always live in the small houses, and the small families in the big houses?" . . .

"I shall give the nine Ruggleses a grand Christmas dinner here in this very room—that will be Papa's contribution—and afterwards a beautiful Christmas tree, fairly blooming with presents—that will be my part; for I have another way of adding to my twenty-five dollars, so that I can buy nearly anything I choose. I should like it very much if you would sit at the head of the table, Uncle Jack, for nobody could ever be frightened of you, you dearest, dearest, dearest thing that ever was! Mamma is going to help us, but Papa and the boys are going to eat together downstairs for fear of making the little Ruggleses shy; and after we've had a merry time with the tree we can open my window and all listen together to the music at the evening church-service, if it comes before the children go. I have written a letter to the organist, and asked him if I might have the two songs I like best. Will you see if it is all right?" . . .

The days flew by as they always fly in holiday time, and it was Christmas Eve before anybody knew it. The family festival was quiet and very pleasant, but almost overshadowed by the grander preparations for the next day. . . .

Mrs. Ruggles was up and stirring about the house, for it was a gala day in the family. Gala day! I should think so! Were not her nine 'childern' invited to a dinner-party at the great house, and weren't they going to sit down free and equal with the mightiest in the land? She had been preparing for this grand occasion ever since the receipt of Carol Bird's invitation. . . .

Bird's Nest, December 17, 188—

Dear Mrs. Ruggles—I am going to have a dinner-party on Christmas Day, and would like to have all your children come. I want them every one, please, from Sarah Maud to Baby Larry. Mamma says dinner will be at half past five, and the Christmas tree at seven; so you may expect them home at nine o'clock. Wishing you a Merry Christmas and a Happy New Year, I am
Yours truly
Carol Bird

Carol's bed had been moved into the farthest corner of the room, and she was lying on the outside, dressed in a wonderful dressing-gown that looked like a fleecy cloud. Her golden hair fell in fluffy curls over her white forehead and neck, her cheeks flushed delicately, her eyes beamed with joy, and the children told their mother, afterwards, that she looked as beautiful as the angels in the picture books.

There was a great bustle behind a huge screen in another part of the room, and at half past five this was taken away, and the Christmas dinnertable stood revealed. What a wonderful sight it was to the poor little Ruggles children, who ate their sometimes scanty meals on the kitchen table! It blazed with tall colored candles, it gleamed with glass and silver, it blushed with flowers, it groaned with good things to eat; so it was not strange that the Ruggleses, forgetting altogether that their mother was a McGrill, shrieked in admiration of the fairy spectacle. . . .

You can well believe that everybody was very merry and very thankful. All the family, from Mr. Bird down to the cook, said

that they had never seen so much happiness in the space of three hours; but it had to end, as all things do. The candles flickered and went out, the tree was left alone with its gilded ornaments, and Mrs. Bird sent the children downstairs at half past eight, thinking that Carol looked tired. . . .

"Can I have the shutters open? and won't you turn my bed, please? This morning I woke ever so early, and one bright, beautiful star shone in that eastern window. I never noticed it before, and I thought of the Star in the East, that guided the wise men to the place where the baby Jesus was. Good-night, Mamma. Such a happy, happy day!"

"Good-night, my precious Christmas Carol—mother's blessed Christmas child."

"Bend your head a minute, mother dear," whispered Carol, calling her mother back. "Mamma, dear, I do think that we have kept Christ's birthday this time just as He would like it. Don't you?"

"I am sure of it," said Mrs. Bird softly.

The Ruggleses had finished a last romp in the library with Paul and Hugh, and Uncle Jack had taken them home and stayed a while to chat with Mrs. Ruggles. . . .

As Uncle Jack went down the rickety steps he looked back into the window for a last glimpse of the family, as the children gathered about their mother, showing their beautiful presents again and again—and then upward to a window in the great house yonder. 'A little child shall lead them,' he thought. "Well, if—if anything every happens to Carol, I will take the Ruggleses under my wing."

"Softly, Uncle Jack," whispered the boys, as he walked into the library a while later. "We are listening to the music in the church. The choir has sung 'Carol, brothers, carol,' and now we think the organist is beginning to play 'My ain countree' for Carol." . . .

I am far frae my hame,
  I am weary aften whiles
For the langed-for hame-bringin',
  An' my Faether's welcome smiles;
An' I'll ne'er be fu' content,
  Until my e'en do see
The gowden gates o' heaven
  In my ain countree.

There were tears in many eyes, but not in Carol's. The loving heart had quietly ceased to beat, and the 'wee birdie' in the great house had flown to its 'home nest.' Carol had fallen asleep! But as to the song, I think perhaps, I cannot say, she heard it after all!

So sad an ending to a happy day! Perhaps—to those who were left; and yet Carol's mother, even in the freshness of her grief, was glad that her darling had slipped away on the loveliest day of her life, out of glad content, into everlasting peace.

She was glad that she had gone as she had come, on the wings of song, when all the world was brimming over with joy; glad of every grateful smile, of every joyous burst of laughter, of every loving thought and word and deed the dear last day had brought. . . .

And so the old years, fraught with memories, die, one after another, and the new years, bright with hopes, are born to take their places; but Carol lives again in every chime of Christmas bells that peal glad tidings, and in every Christmas anthem sung by childish voices.

Dear Santa

Dear Santa, please note
That on Christmas this year,
There's a new little fellow
We all hold so dear,
He's tiny and precious
And can't understand
The gladness of holding
A toy in his hand.

Dear Santa, I'm writing
'Cause he's much too small,
A wee little angel
Not quite a yard tall,
But, oh, he's so precious,
His face wrapped in smiles;
He's all of our Christmas;
He loves and beguiles.

Dear Santa, his stocking
Is so very wee,
Perhaps you shall miss it
Beneath the huge tree,
But do treat it gently
And leave him a toy,
For though he's quite tiny
He's our pride and joy.

He's loving and happy,
So much joy he gives;
His heart filled with laughter
Each day that he lives.
We've told him you're coming,
Of presents and cheer;
We're certain, dear Santa,
He'll know you next year.

Garnett Ann Schultz

From
A Christmas Carol

Charles Dickens

Then up rose Mrs. Cratchit, Cratchit's wife, dressed out but poorly in a twice-turned gown, but brave in ribbons, which are cheap, and make a goodly show for sixpence; and she laid the cloth, assisted by Belinda Cratchit, second of her daughters, also brave in ribbons; while Master Peter Cratchit plunged a fork into the saucepan of potatoes, and getting the corners of his monstrous shirtcollar (Bob's private property, conferred upon his son and heir in honor of the day) into his mouth, rejoiced to find himself so gallantly attired, and yearned to show his linen in the fashionable Parks.

And now two smaller Cratchits, boy and girl, came tearing in screaming that outside the baker's they had smelled the goose, and known it for their own; and basking in luxurious thoughts of sage and onion, these young Cratchits danced about the table, and exalted Master Peter Cratchit to the skies, while he (not proud, although his collars nearly choked him) blew the fire, until the slow potatoes, bubbling up, knocked loudly at the saucepan lid to be let out and peeled.

"What has ever got your precious father, then?" said Mrs. Cratchit. "And your brother, Tiny Tim? And Martha warn't as late last Christmas Day by half an hour!"

"Here's Martha, Mother," said a girl, appearing as she spoke.

"Here's Martha, Mother!" cried the two young Cratchits.

"Hurrah! There's such a goose, Martha!"

"Why, bless your heart alive, my dear, how late you are!" said Mrs. Cratchit, kissing her a dozen times, and taking off her shawl and bonnet for her with officious zeal.

"We'd a deal of work to finish up last night," replied the girl, "and had to clear away this morning, Mother!"

"Well! Never mind so long as you are come," said Mrs. Cratchit. "Sit ye down before the fire, my dear, and have a warm, Lord bless ye!"

"No, no! There's Father coming," cried the two young Cratchits, who were everywhere at once. "Hide, Martha, hide!"

So Martha hid herself, and in came little Bob, the father, with at least three feet of comforter, exclusive of the fringe, hanging down before him, and his threadbare clothes darned up and brushed to look seasonable, and

Tiny Tim upon his shoulders. Alas for Tiny Tim, he bore a little crutch, and had his limbs supported by an iron frame!

"Why, where's our Martha?" cried Bob Cratchit, looking around.

"Not coming," said Mrs. Cratchit.

"Not coming!" said Bob, with a sudden declension in his high spirits; for he had been Tim's blood-horse all the way from church and had come home rampant. "Not coming upon Christmas Day!"

Martha didn't like to see him disappointed, if it were only in joke; so she came out prematurely from behind the closet door, and ran into his arms, while the two young Cratchits hustled Tiny Tim, and bore him off into the washhouse, that he might hear the pudding singing in the copper.

"And how did little Tim behave?" asked Mrs. Cratchit, when she had rallied Bob on his credulity, and Bob had hugged his daughter to his heart's content.

"As good as gold," said Bob, "and better. Somehow he gets thoughtful, sitting by himself so much, and thinks the strangest things you ever heard. He told me, coming home, that he hoped the people saw him in the church, because he was a cripple, and it might be pleasant to them to remember upon Christmas Day who made lame beggars walk and blind men see."

Bob's voice was tremulous when he told them this, and trembled more when he said that Tiny Tim was growing strong and hearty.

His active little crutch was heard upon the floor, and back came Tiny Tim before another word was spoken, escorted by his brother and sister to his stool beside the fire; and while Bob, turning up his cuffs—as if, poor fellow, they were capable of being made more shabby—compounded some hot mixture in a jug with gin and lemons, and stirred it round and round, and put it on the hob to simmer, Master Peter and the two ubiquitous young Cratchits went to fetch the goose, with which they soon returned in high procession.

Such a bustle ensued that you might have thought a goose the rarest of all birds; a feathered phenomenon, to which a black swan was a matter of course—and in truth, it was something very like it in that house.

Mrs. Cratchit made the gravy (ready beforehand in a little saucepan) hissing hot; Master Peter mashed the potatoes with incredible vigor; Miss Belinda sweetened up the applesauce; Martha dusted the hot plates; Bob took Tiny Tim beside him in a tiny corner at the table; the two young Cratchits set chairs for everyone, not forgetting themselves, and, mounting guard upon their posts, crammed spoons into their mouths, lest they should shriek for goose before their turn came to be helped.

At last the dishes were set on, and grace was said. It was succeeded by a breathless pause, as Mrs. Cratchit, looking slowly all along the carving knife, prepared to plunge it in the breast; but when she did, and when the long-expected gush of stuffing issued forth, one murmur

of delight arose all round the board, and even Tiny Tim, excited by the two young Cratchits, beat on the table with the handle of his knife and feebly cried Hurrah!

There never was such a goose. Bob said he didn't believe there ever was such a goose cooked. Its tenderness and flavor, size and cheapness, were the themes of universal admiration. Eked out by applesauce and mashed potatoes, it was a sufficient dinner for the whole family; indeed, as Mrs. Cratchit said with great delight (surveying one small atom of a bone upon the dish), they hadn't ate it all at last! Yet every one had enough, and the youngest Cratchits, in particular, were steeped in sage and onion to the eyebrows! But now, the plates being changed by Miss Belinda, Mrs. Cratchit left the room alone—too nervous to bear witnesses to take the pudding up, and bring it in.

Suppose it should not be done enough! Suppose it should break in turning out! Suppose somebody should have got over the wall of the backyard and stolen it, while they were merry with the goose—a supposition at which the two young Cratchits became livid! All sorts of horrors were supposed.

Hallo! A great deal of steam! the pudding was out of the copper. A smell like a washing day! That was the cloth. A smell like an eating house and a pastry cook's next door to each other, with a laundress's next door to that! That was the pudding.

In a half a minute Mrs. Cratchit entered—flushed, but smiling proudly—with the pudding, like a speckled cannonball, so hard and firm, blazing in half of half-a-quartern of ignited brandy, and bedight with Christmas holly stuck into the top.

Oh, a wonderful pudding! Bob Cratchit said, and calmly, too, that he regarded it as the greatest success achieved by Mrs. Cratchit since their marriage. Mrs. Cratchit said that, now the weight was off her mind, she would confess she had her doubts about the quantity of flour. Everybody had something to say about it, but nobody said or thought it was at all a small pudding for a large family. It would have been flat heresy to do so. Any Cratchit would have blushed to hint at such a thing.

At last the dinner was all done, the cloth was cleared, the hearth swept, and the fire made up. The compound in the jug being tasted, and considered perfect, apples and oranges were put upon the table, and a shovelful of chestnuts on the fire. Then all the Cratchit family drew round the hearth in what Bob Cratchit called a circle, meaning half a one, and at Bob Cratchit's elbow stood the family display of glass. Two tumblers and a custard-cup without a handle. These held the hot stuff from the jug, however, as well as golden goblets would have done; and Bob served it out with beaming looks, while the chestnuts on the fire sputtered and cracked noisily. Then Bob proposed:

"A Merry Christmas to us all, my dears. God bless us!"

Which all the family re-echoed.

"God bless us every one!" said Tiny Tim, the last of all.

A Child's Wish for Christmas

I wish there were
A giant Christmas tree—
So tall its lights
Would shine around the earth
For all to see,
The happy and the sad,
The poor and humble,
Those of royal birth.

The Christmas star
Would be there at the top;
Its glorious light
Would melt the coldest heart,
Make men forget
Their hatreds and their greed,
Clasp hands in friendship
And from wars depart.

This world would then
The Christmas story share
And know the joy
That came to Bethlehem
That night, when
Christ the Lord was born—
The Prince of Peace,
God's gift of love to men.

Linnea Englund Reed

The Day After the Night Before Christmas

The children were stirring,
A new day was born.
They jumped from their beds
To greet Christmas morn.

The tiny mouse, sleeping
In his snug retreat,
Was wakened by laughter
And pattering feet.

They ran to the window
And saw with delight
The tracks that a big sleigh
Had made in the night.

As bright eyes, still sleepy,
Watched roof and below,
The tracks were soon covered
With new falling snow.

Smiles lit shining faces,
'Twas now getting light,
For Santa had brought them
A Christmas all white.

They scurried for housecoats,
Found slippers in pairs,
With little feet flying
They raced down the stairs.

The tiny mouse watched them,
Then, bold as you please,
Came out of his haven
To look for some cheese.

The children's eyes sparkled
For, lo and behold,
Their Christmas tree glistened
With silver and gold.

The stockings were filled up,
Near touching the floor,
In front of the fireplace
With presents galore.

They looked at the mantel
Where dear Santa's lunch
Had been on a big plate
With good things to munch.

The plate was quite empty;
On top was a note.
It surely must be one
That Santa Claus wrote.

Too high for the children,
Way over each head,
They waited for Father
To read what it said.

While they all still wondered
The stairs gave a creak.
Both Mom and Dad smiled as
They came in to peek.

Warm kisses were given
By Dad and Mother.
'Twas a loving Christmas
Wished to each other.

Dad reached for the letter,
Each word was read slow.
"My Christmas Eve supper
Was tasty. Ho! Ho!"

Dear Dad went on reading,
"My thanks one and all.
Your white Christmas snowflakes
Will soon start to fall!"

The children said, laughing,
"It's started to snow,
Like Santa Claus promised
When he wrote, 'Ho! Ho!'"

Bright papers went flying
As ribbons came free.
The stockings were emptied
Amid shouts of glee.

Two bright eyes were shining
From a small corner.
'Twas the brave tiny mouse,
Just like Jack Horner.

Another small stocking
Still hung from the tree
As tippy-toed children
Reached high up to see.

The tiny mouse knew that
He'd been good all year.
The stocking must be his.
There's nothing to fear.

He ran to the children
And said, "Pretty please,
And thanks to dear Santa."
His stocking held cheese.

The mouse joined the family,
As each one gave thanks,
And promised that next year
He would not play pranks!

James L. Moore

Best Christmas Gift

He rushed down the stairs,
　Anxious to see
What Santa had left
　Neath the gay tree.

He opened each package
　Mid squeals of delight;
Each gift he received
　Was shiny and bright.

His heart's special wish
　Was not to be found,
When all of a sudden
　He heard a strange sound;

There in the stocking
　Carefully hung up,
All snuggly and warm
　Was a cute little pup.

No gift he received
　Held quite so much charm
As that wee little puppy
　Held close in his arms.

With so much excitement
　Filling his head,
He took his best gift
　And trudged back to bed!

Kay Hoffman

Her Precious Gift

She looked at the tree, her little girl eyes
Lighted with wonder and glad surprise.

"Oh, Mother, the tree's so pretty!" she said,
In a voice like a song. Then turning her head,
She saw the basket where you were curled,
And all the Christmas trees in the world
Were not as shining and candle-bright
As her face that mirrored a gold delight.

She lifted you up, too happy to speak,
And held you close to her warm young cheek.
Then stroked your fur, your ribbon of blue,
And a heartful of love flowed out to you.
The dearest gift that a child could know . . .
The Christmas kitten she wanted so.

Grace V. Watkins

Let Us Keep Christmas

Grace Noll Crowell

Whatever else be lost among the years,
    Let us keep Christmas still a shining thing.
Whatever doubts assail us, or what fears,
    Let us hold close one day, remembering
Its poignant meaning for the hearts of men.
    Let us get back our childlike faith again.

Wealth may have taken wings, yet still there are
    Clear windowpanes to glow with candlelight;
There are boughs for garlands, and a tinsel star
    To tip some little fir tree's lifted height.
There is no heart too heavy or too sad,
    But some small gift of love can make it glad.

And there are home-sweet rooms where laughter rings,
    And we can sing the carols as of old;
Above the eastern hills a white star swings;
    There is an ancient story to be told;
There are kind words and cheering words to say.
    Let us be happy on the Christ Child's day.

"Let Us Keep Christmas" from POEMS OF INSPIRATION AND COURAGE by Grace Noll Crowell. Copyright 1950 by Grace Noll Crowell. Reprinted by permission of Harper & Row, Publishers, Inc.

Of Christmas

Sing a song of Christmas,
Of stockings full of toys,
Stuffed by dear old Santa
For all good girls and boys.

Sing a song of Christmas,
Of puddings made with spice;
Of hungry lads and lassies
Who beg a second slice.

Sing a song of Christmas
Of holly, green and red;
Of crisp and snowy weather.
That calls for skate and sled.

Sing a song of Christmas
Of carols sweet and gay,
That tell of old Judea
Where Infant Jesus lay.

Sing a song of Christmas,
May laughter, love and cheer
Possess our hearts this blessed day,
And through the coming year.

Grace L. Schauffler

The Music of Christmas

What Child Is This?

What Child is this who laid to rest
On Mary's lap is sleeping,
Whom angels greet with anthems sweet
While shepherds watch are keeping?
This, this is Christ the King
Whom shepherds guard and angels sing,
Haste, haste to bring him laud,
The Babe, the Son of Mary.

Why lies he in such mean estate
Where ox and ass are feeding?
Good Christian fear, for sinners here
The silent word is pleading.
Nails, spear shall pierce him through.
The cross be borne for me, for you.
Hail, hail, the Lord made flesh,
The Babe, the Son of Mary.

So bring him incense, gold and myrrh,
Come peasant, king to own him.
The King of kings salvation brings,
Let loving hearts enthrone him.
Raise, raise the song on high,
The virgin sings her lullaby,
Joy, joy for Christ is born,
The Babe, the Son of Mary.

W.C. Dix

Silent Night! Holy Night!

Silent night! holy night!
All is calm, all is bright;
Round yon virgin mother and Child,
Holy Infant so tender and mild;
Sleep in heavenly peace,
Sleep in heavenly peace.

Silent night! holy night!
Darkness flies, all is light;
Shepherds hear the angels sing:
"Alleluia! hail the King!
Christ the Savior is born,
Christ the Savior is born."

Silent night! holy night!
Guiding Star, lend thy light!
See the eastern wise men bring
Gifts and homage to our King!
Christ the Savior is born,
Christ the Savior is born.

Silent night! holy night!
Wondrous Star, lend thy light!
With the angels let us sing
Alleluia to our King!
Christ the Savior is born,
Christ the Savior is born.

Joseph Mohr

Good King Wenceslaus

Good King Wenceslaus looked out
On the Feast of Stephen,
When the snow lay round about,
Deep, and crisp, and even.

Brightly shone the moon that night
Though the frost was cruel,
When a poor man came in sight,
Gath'ring winter fuel.

"Hither, page, and stand by me,
If thou know'st it, telling,
Yonder peasant, who is he?
Where and what his dwelling?"

"Sire, he lives a good league hence,
Underneath the mountain;
Right against the forest fence,
By Saint Agnes' fountain."

"Bring me flesh, and bring me wine,
Bring me pine logs hither;
Thou and I shall see him dine,
When we bear them thither."

Page and monarch, forth they went,
Forth they went together;
Through the rude wind's wild lament
And the bitter weather.

"Sire, the night is darker now,
And the wind blows stronger;
Fails my heart, I know not how,
I can go no longer."

"Mark my footsteps, good my page;
Tread thou in them boldly:
Thou shalt find the winter rage
Freeze thy blood less coldly."

In his master's steps he trod,
Where the snow lay dinted;
Heat was in the very sod
Where the saint had printed.

Therefore, Christian men, be sure,
Wealth or rank possessing,
Ye who now will bless the poor,
Shall yourselves find blessing.
Translaslated from the Latin by J.M. Neale

Hark! the Herald Angels Sing

Hark! the herald angels sing,
"Glory to the newborn King;
Peace on earth, and mercy mild,
God and sinners reconciled!"
Joyful all ye nations rise,
Join the triumph of the skies;
With th' angelic host proclaim,
"Christ is born in Bethlehem."
Hark! the herald angels sing,
"Glory to the newborn King."

Christ, by highest heaven adored;
Christ, the everlasting Lord;
Come, Desire of Nations, come,
Fix in us thy humble home.
Veiled in flesh the Godhead see;
Hail th' Incarnate Deity,
Pleased as man with men to dwell;
Jesus, our Emmanuel.
Hark! the herald angels sing,
"Glory to the newborn King."

Hail, the heaven-born Prince of Peace!
Hail, the Sun of Righteousness!
Light and life to all he brings,
Risen with healing in his wings.
Mild he lays his glory by.
Born that man no more may die,
Born to raise the sons of earth,
Born to give them second birth.
Hark! the herald angels sing,
"Glory to the newborn King."
Charles Wesley

Away in a Manger

Away in a manger, no crib for a bed,
The little Lord Jesus lay down his sweet head.
The stars in the sky looked down where he lay,
The little Lord Jesus, asleep on the hay.

The cattle are lowing, the Baby awakes,
But little Lord Jesus, no crying he makes.
I love thee, Lord Jesus, look down from the sky,
And stay by my cradle till morning is nigh.

Be near me, Lord Jesus, I ask thee to stay
Close by me forever, and love me, I pray.
Bless all the dear children in thy tender care,
And fit us for heaven to live with thee there.
Martin Luther

Christmas
ISSUE

ideals

Ideals' Pages
from the Past

On the following six pages,
we are presenting a selection
from Christmas Ideals 1951.

Hello, Again

Nina Gertrude Smith

Hello, again, it's Christmas!
In the postman's ring
In a little child's face
On the snowbird's wing;

In the "sh-sh-sh" of secrets;
Colors, sounds and smells—
In a stranger's warm sweet laughter
Hear the golden bells!

Christmas in the sacred story
Of a Yuletide's song,
In a new re-captured glory
Righting every wrong.

In the joy of giving, giving . . .
Christmas in the air;
Faith and hope and love are living—
Christmas, Christmas, everywhere!

CHRISTMAS FANTASY

Lola Taylor Hemphill

The Pixies and the Brownies
   all go up North, I hear,
To lend a hand to Santa
   about this time each year —

*For he needs lots of helpers
   with books and games and toys,
To carry over all the world
   to little girls and boys.*

Now — his merry little helpers
   are 'bout your size, I s'pose —
With twinkling eyes and smiling lips,
   and oh! the gayest clothes;

*And they whistle, laugh, and chatter
   in a happy sort of way;
Because they know the fun in store
   for you on Christmas Day!*

But then — before the time arrives
   to pack up Santa's sleigh,
They have so many things to do
   they work 'most night and day.

*They have to shine the gold sleigh bells,
   and get them all in tune,
So they will jingle lovely songs
   beneath the Christmas moon;*

They brush each furry reindeer coat,
   and tend each tiny hoof,
For they must carry Santa
   to every snow-capped roof;

The Brownies feed them fresh, sweet hay,
   and whisper in each ear
That time has come for that long trip
   they make just once each year.

And then, they polish all the horns
   upon each reindeer head,
And decorate the harness
   with silver, green and red.

Next, they bring out Santa's mittens,
   and his great red fur-trimmed suit;
And a dozen of the little men
   drag out his shining boots:

And after they have dressed him,
   they bring for him to drink
A big warm mug of chocolate, —
   it must be good, I think!

Now — everything is ready,
   so they tuck him in the sleigh,
And wait the magic moment
   when he will start away;

Old Santa gives a chuckle, —
   and the reindeer proudly prance,
Then to the music of the bells
   the wee men start to dance —

And with words known just to Pixies,
   so light and rollicking,
A merry little Christmas tune
   they all begin to sing, —

And Santa calls this message
   as he swiftly slips away:
"I'll see all the children
   have a Merry Christmas Day!"

A Legend

There's a beautiful legend
That's never been told —
It may have been known
To the Wise Men of old —
How three little children
Came early at dawn,
With hearts that were sad
To where Jesus was born.

One could not see,
One was too lame to play;
While the other, a mute
Not a word could he say.
Yet, led by His Star,
They came there to peep
At the little Lord Jesus
With eyes closed in sleep.

But how could the Christ Child,
So lovely and fair,
Not waken and smile
When He heard their glad prayer,
Of hope at His coming,
Of faith in His birth,
Of praise at His bringing
God's peace to the earth?

And, then, as the light
Softly came through the door,
The lad that was lame
Stood upright once more.
The boy that was mute
Started sweetly to sing —
While the child that was blind
Looked with joy on the King!

*Our sincere thanks to
the unknown author.*

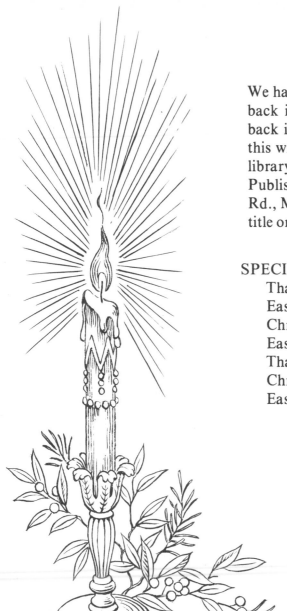

We have received several requests from our readers asking for back issues of Ideals. With that in mind, we have listed the back issues of Ideals which are currently available. We trust this will allow you the opportunity to complete your personal library or order as a gift for any occasion. Write: Ideals Publishing Corporation, Dept. 100, 11315 Watertown Plank Rd., Milwaukee, Wisconsin 53201. Include just $3.00 for each title ordered. Postage and mailing will be included in this price.

SPECIAL HOLIDAY ISSUES
Thanksgiving Ideals '76
Easter Ideals '77
Christmas Ideals '77
Easter Ideals '78
Thanksgiving Ideals '78
Christmas Ideals '78
Easter Ideals '79

POPULAR FAVORITES
Adventure Ideals '76
Memory Ideals '76
Inspiration Ideals '77
Happiness Ideals '77
Woodland Ideals '77
Autumn Time Ideals '77
Fireside Ideals '78
Neighborly Ideals '78
Countryside Ideals '78

COLOR ART AND PHOTO CREDITS:
(in order of appearance)

Cover #1, H. Armstrong Roberts; Cover #2, Poinsettias, Gerald Koser; CHRISTMAS TREE, Yosemite Valley National Park, Calif., Josef Muench; WINTER CHARM, Yosemite Valley National Park, Calif., Josef Muench; Winter sleigh ride, Fred Sieb; Snow-crowned landscape, Robert Holland; Christmas dinner, Three Lions, Inc.; The Christmas hearth, Ralph Luedtke; Yuletide joy, Fred Sieb; HOLY FAMILY, by Francesco Mancini (1679-1758), Three Lions, Inc.; Chapel in Klais, Bavaria, Germany, Tony Stone Associates Ltd.; INNKEEPERS SON, painting by Joseph Maniscalco; ADORATION OF THE THREE KINGS, painting by Joseph Maniscalco; Christmas candle, Gerald Koser; A child's Christmas tree, by Ron Ceszynski; A Christmas greeting, Alpha Photo Inc.; An old-fashioned Christmas, Fred Sieb; Christmas sweets, Fred Sieb; THE TOYMAKER, painting by Norman Rockwell; WAITING FOR SANTA, Three Lions, Inc.; A letter from Carolyn, Ralph Luedtke; A child's wish, Alpha Photo Inc.; Puppy and kitten, H. Armstrong Roberts; Jingle bells, Fred Sieb; CAROLERS, painting by George Hinke; Christmas angels, painting by Miki; Cover #3, Gerald Koser; Cover #4, Gerald Koser.

ACKNOWLEDGMENTS

HANDEL'S CHRISTMAS MASTERPIECE by Marie King. From THE GOLD STAR FAMILY ALBUM, Copyright © 1968. Used with permission of DeMoss Associates. KALEIDOSCOPE by Elizabeth Searle Lamb. From TODAY AND EVERY DAY, Copyright © 1970 by Unity School of Christianity. Used with permission of the author. THE DAY AFTER THE NIGHT BEFORE CHRISTMAS by James L. Moore. Copyright © 1979 by James L. Moore. Used with permission. Excerpt from THE BIRDS' CHRISTMAS CAROL by Kate Douglas Wiggin, published by Houghton Mifflin Company. Our sincere thanks to the following author whose address we were unable to locate: Grace L. Schauffler for OF CHRISTMAS.